The Rescue Series

GRACIE AND HER WOOBIE

Book 4

Paula Gehring-Kevish

Copyright © 2022 Paula Gehring-Kevish
All rights reserved
First Edition

PAGE PUBLISHING, INC.
Conneaut Lake, PA

First originally published by Page Publishing 2022

ISBN 978-1-6624-6325-9 (pbk)
ISBN 978-1-6624-7716-4 (hc)
ISBN 978-1-6624-6326-6 (digital)

Printed in the United States of America

This book is dedicated to the memory of our beloved Lab, Rusty, who will always be in our hearts.

Also by Paula Gehring-Kevish

The Rescue Series:

*The Big Adventures
  of Little Lucky*
Gunner Gets a Forever Home
Mischievous Misti
Gracie and her Woobie

The Courageous
Kids Series:

*The World According
  to Lindsey*

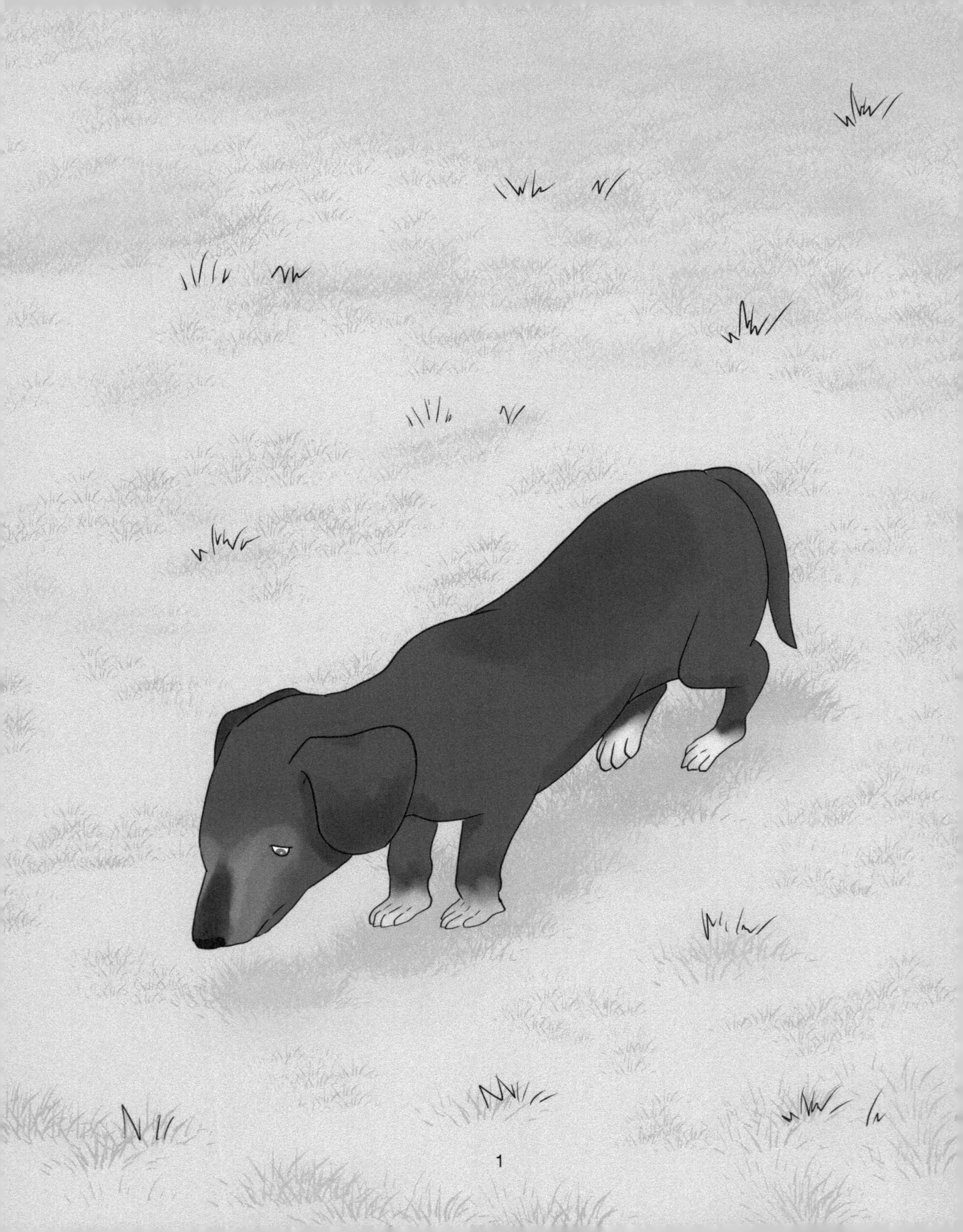

First, let me introduce Gracie. Gracie was the first doxie to join our family.

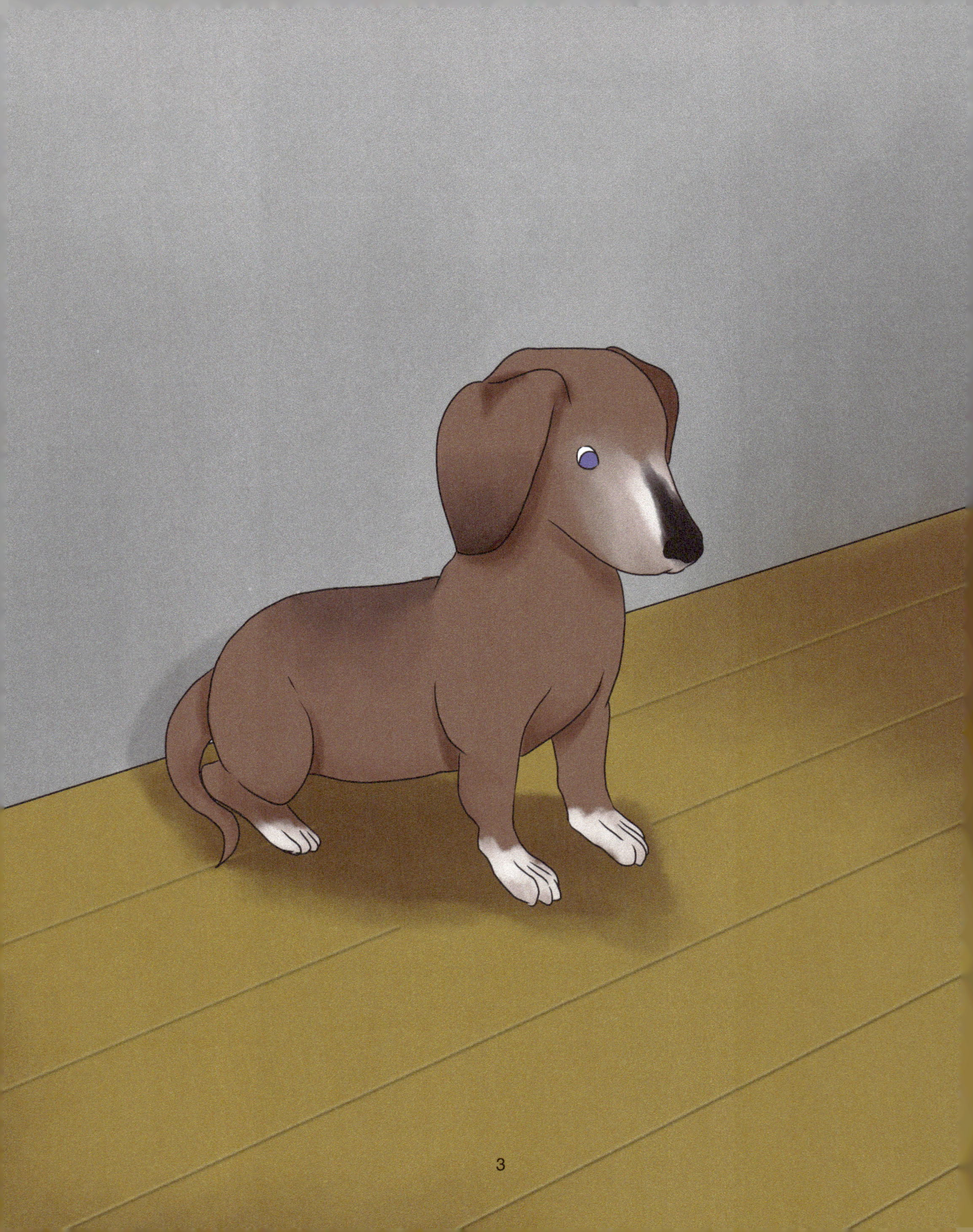

Our kids wanted a puppy, but there were none to find.

We found a newspaper ad saying there was an eight-month-old doxie who needed a new home. We decided to go meet her.

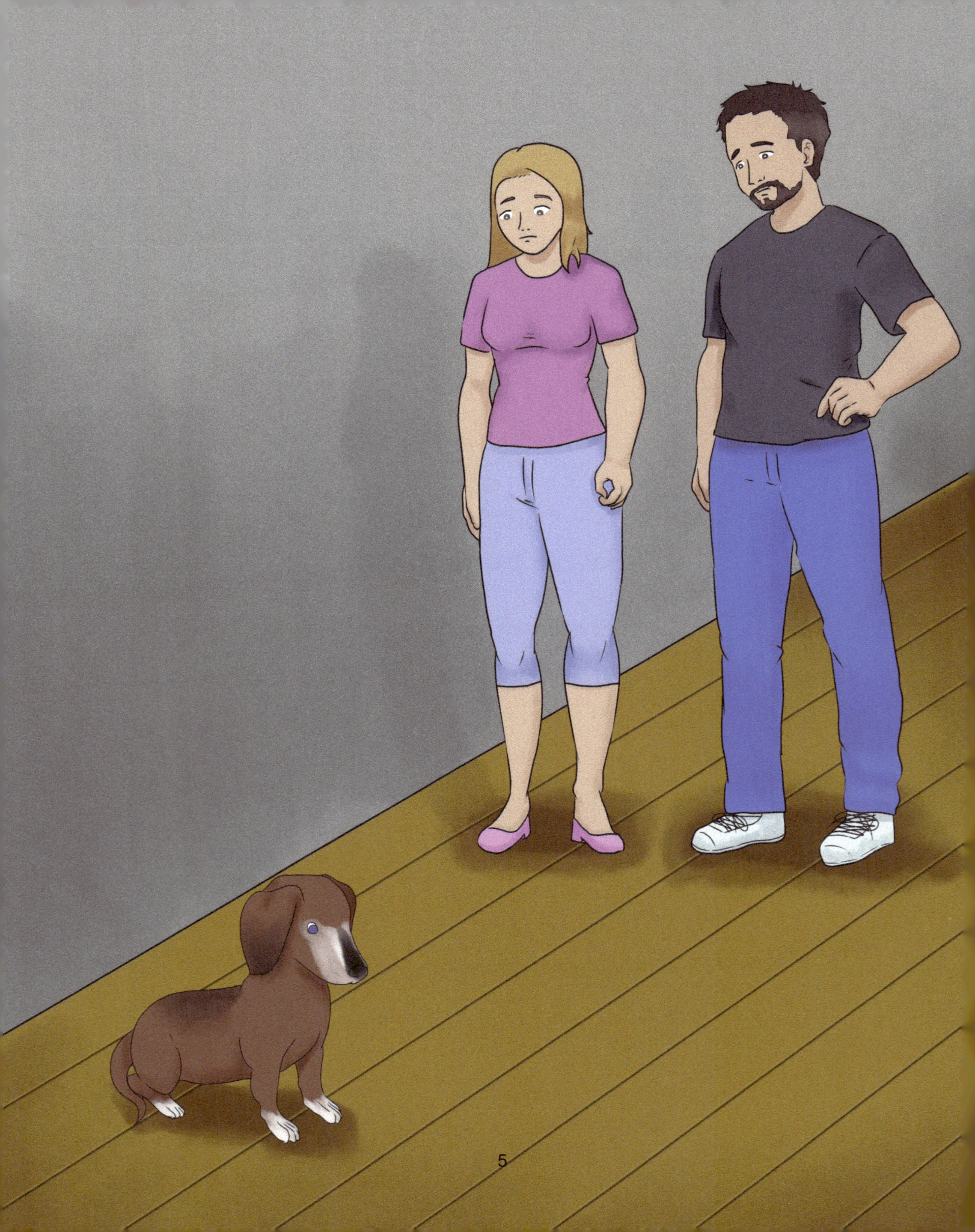

When we first met Gracie, she kept her head down and her tail tucked.

She didn't look at anyone. She just stood in the middle of the room. She looked very sad.

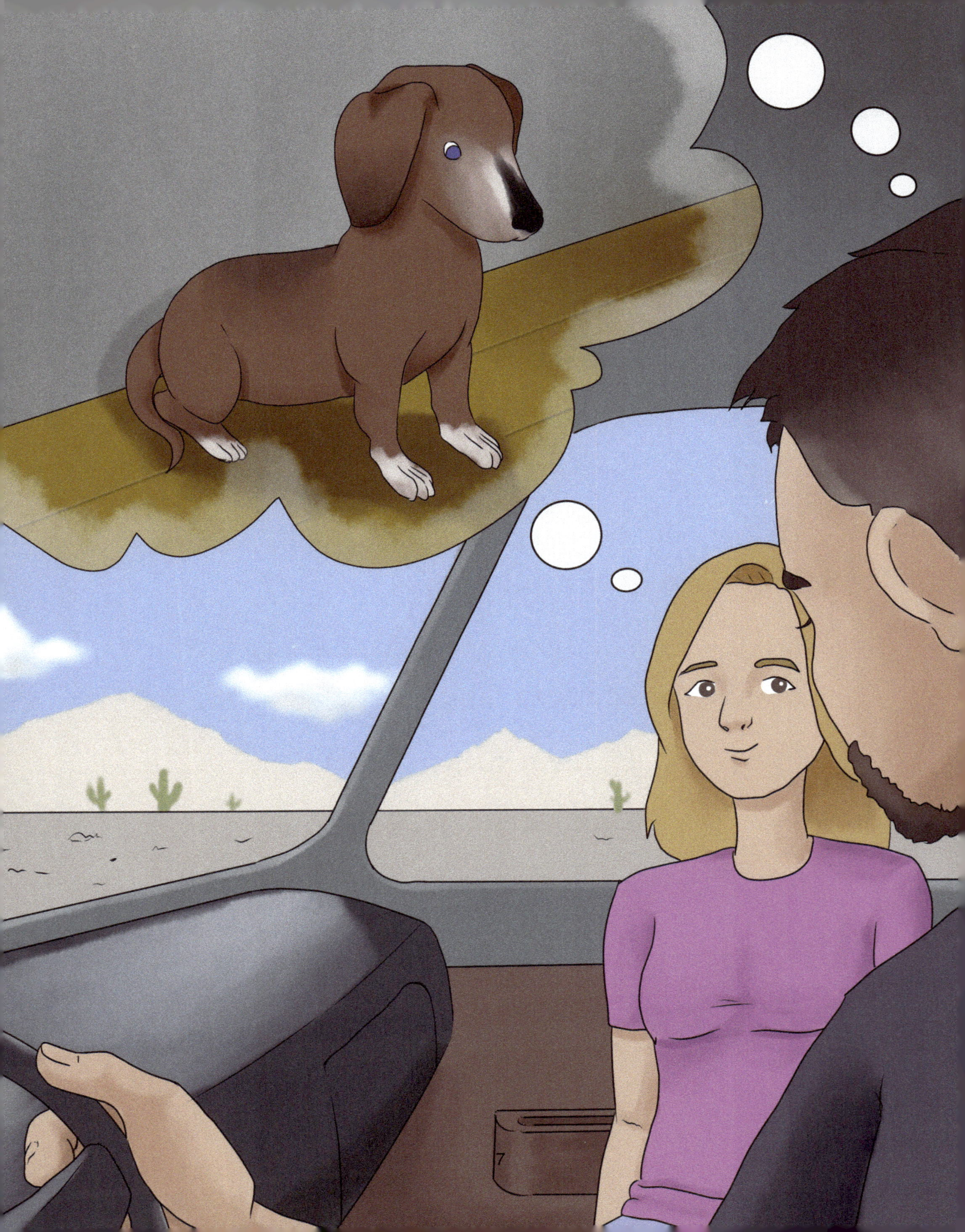

We left without her. We decided in the car that she would be a great addition to our family.

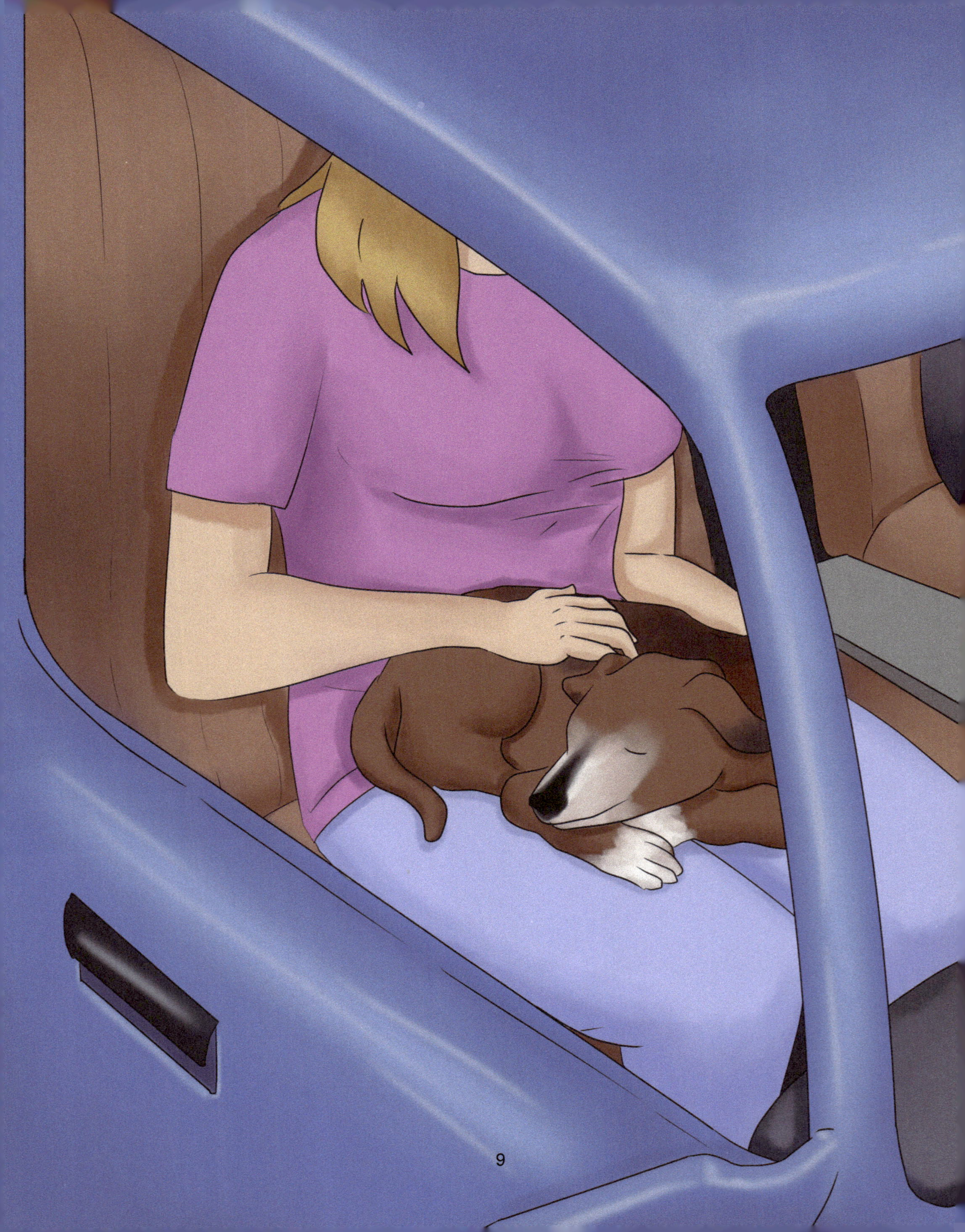

The day we picked up Gracie, we had to make a long road trip. Gracie slept the entire trip.

When we came back, we took Gracie to the pet store and picked out a toy for her to play with.

She picked her purple woobie.

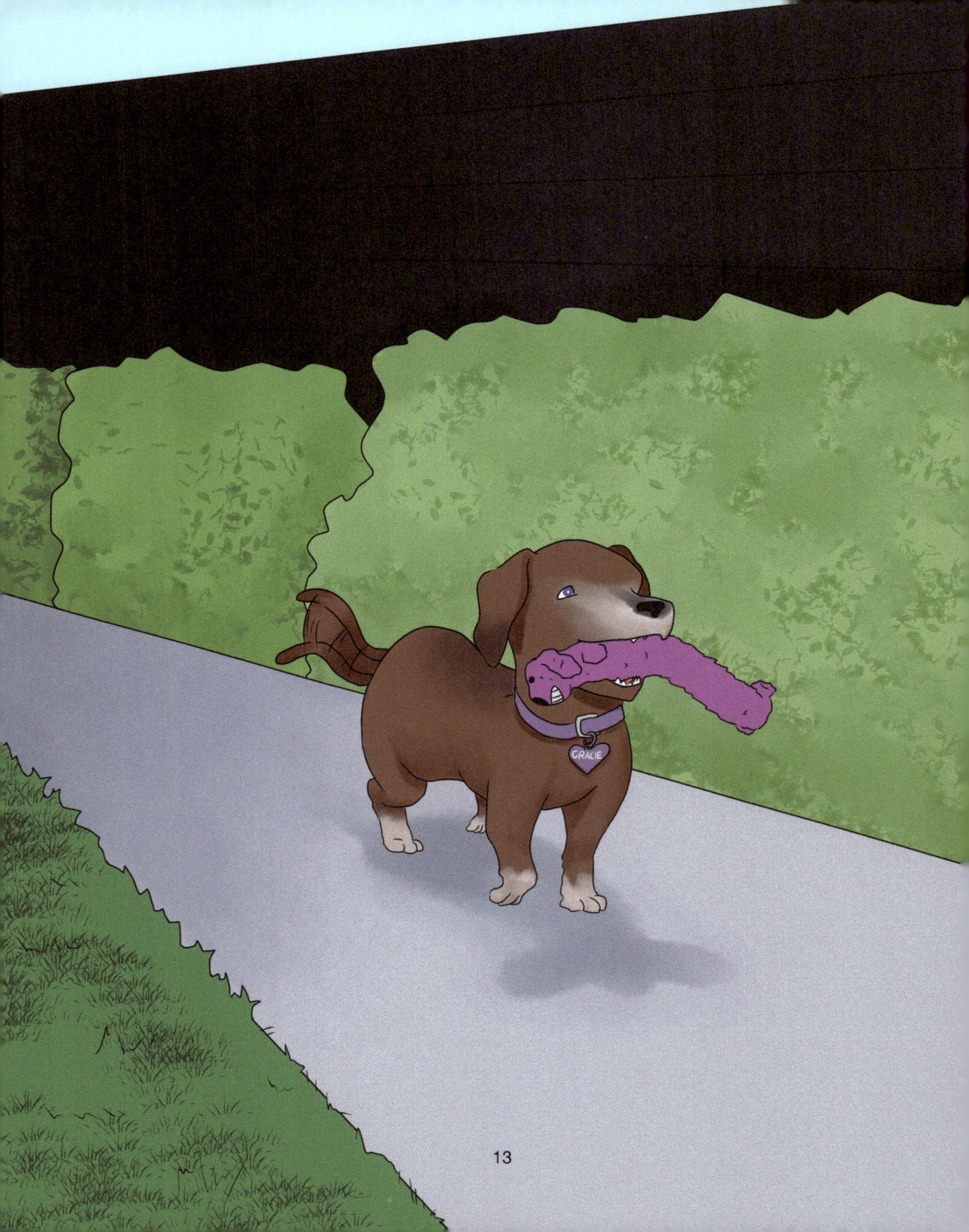
GRACIE

Gracie took her woobie everywhere—to bed,

to every room,

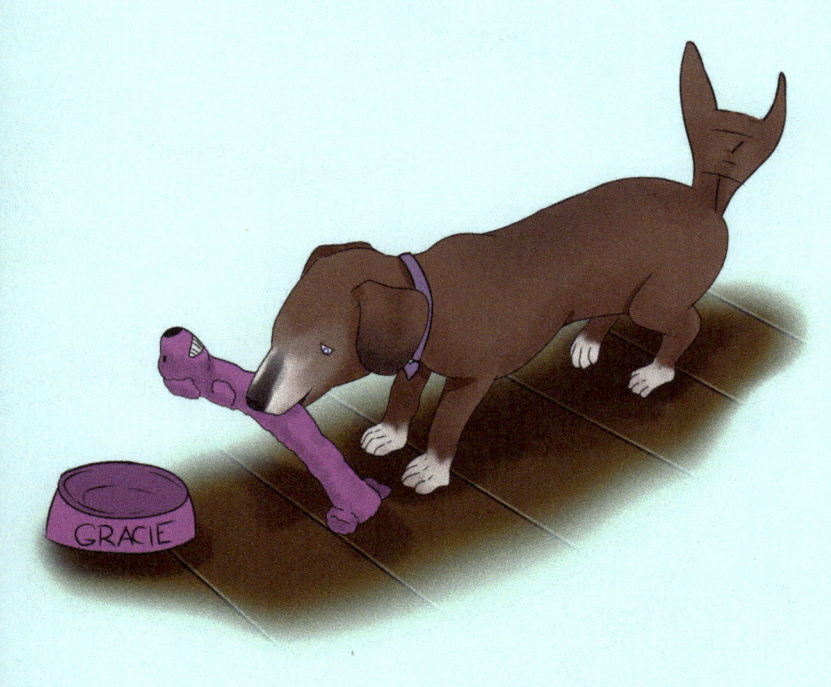

to her bowl when she ate.

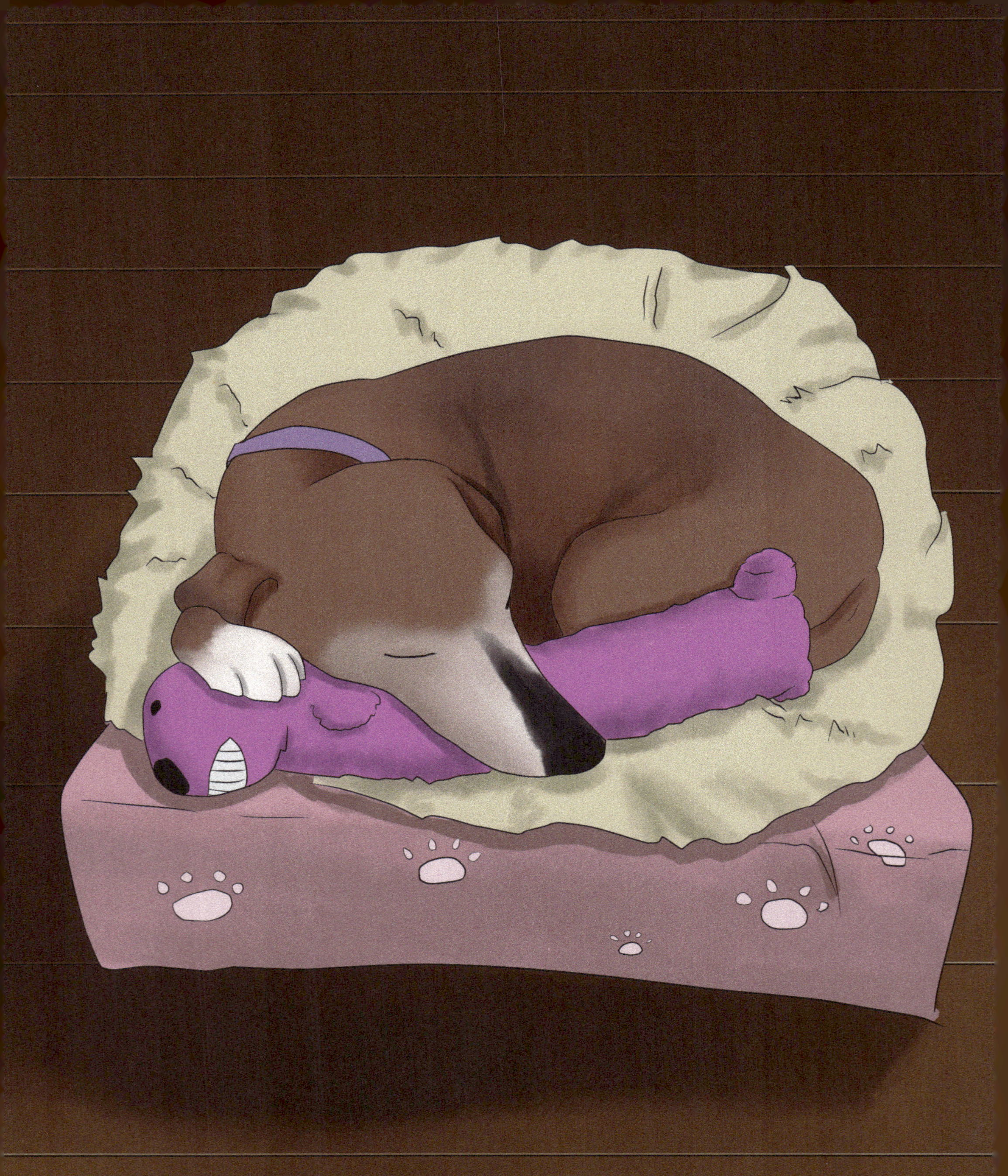

Gracie always slept with it under her head and one leg.

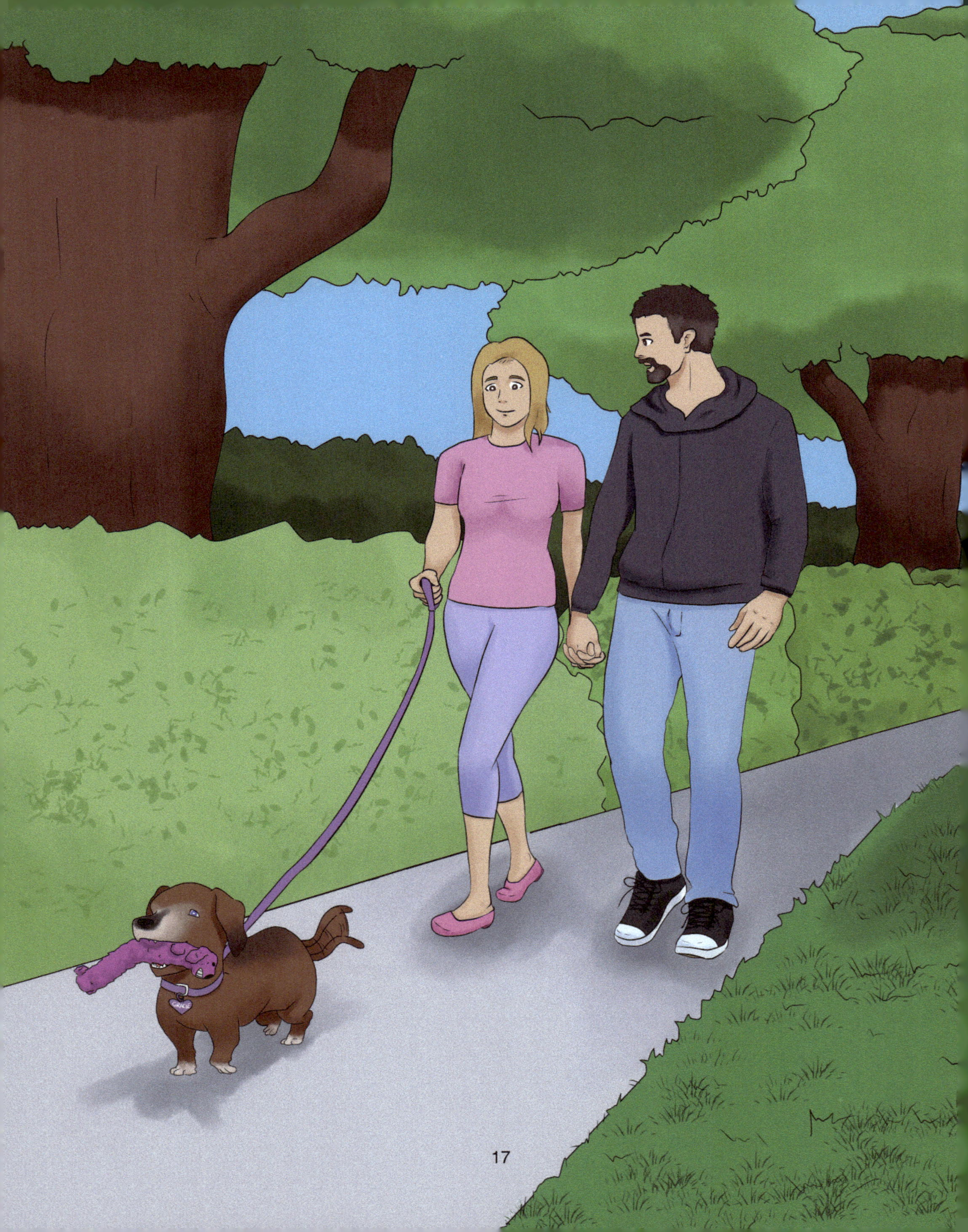

She never leaves it anywhere. If you take Gracie on a walk, she brings her woobie.

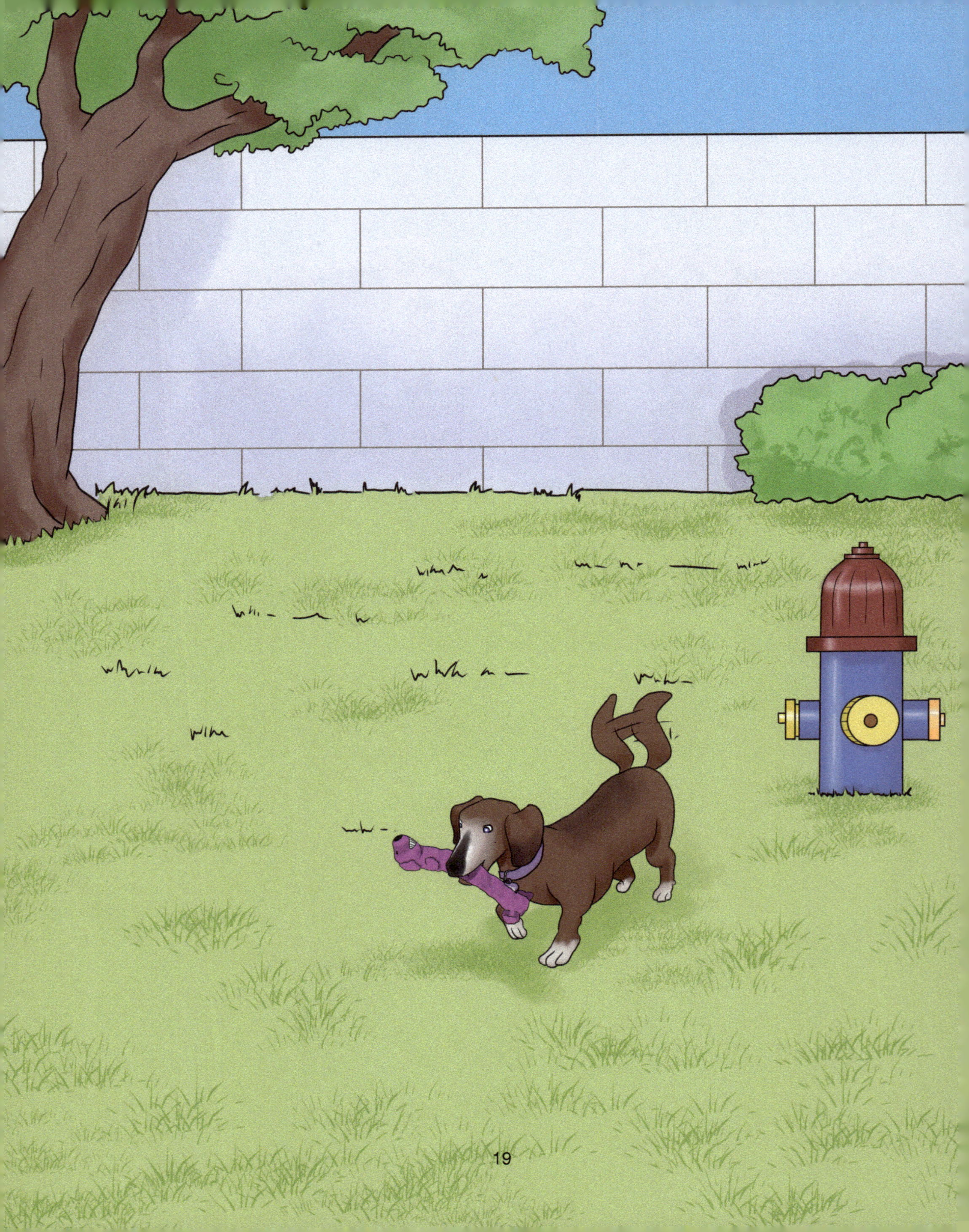

If she goes in the backyard, she brings her woobie.

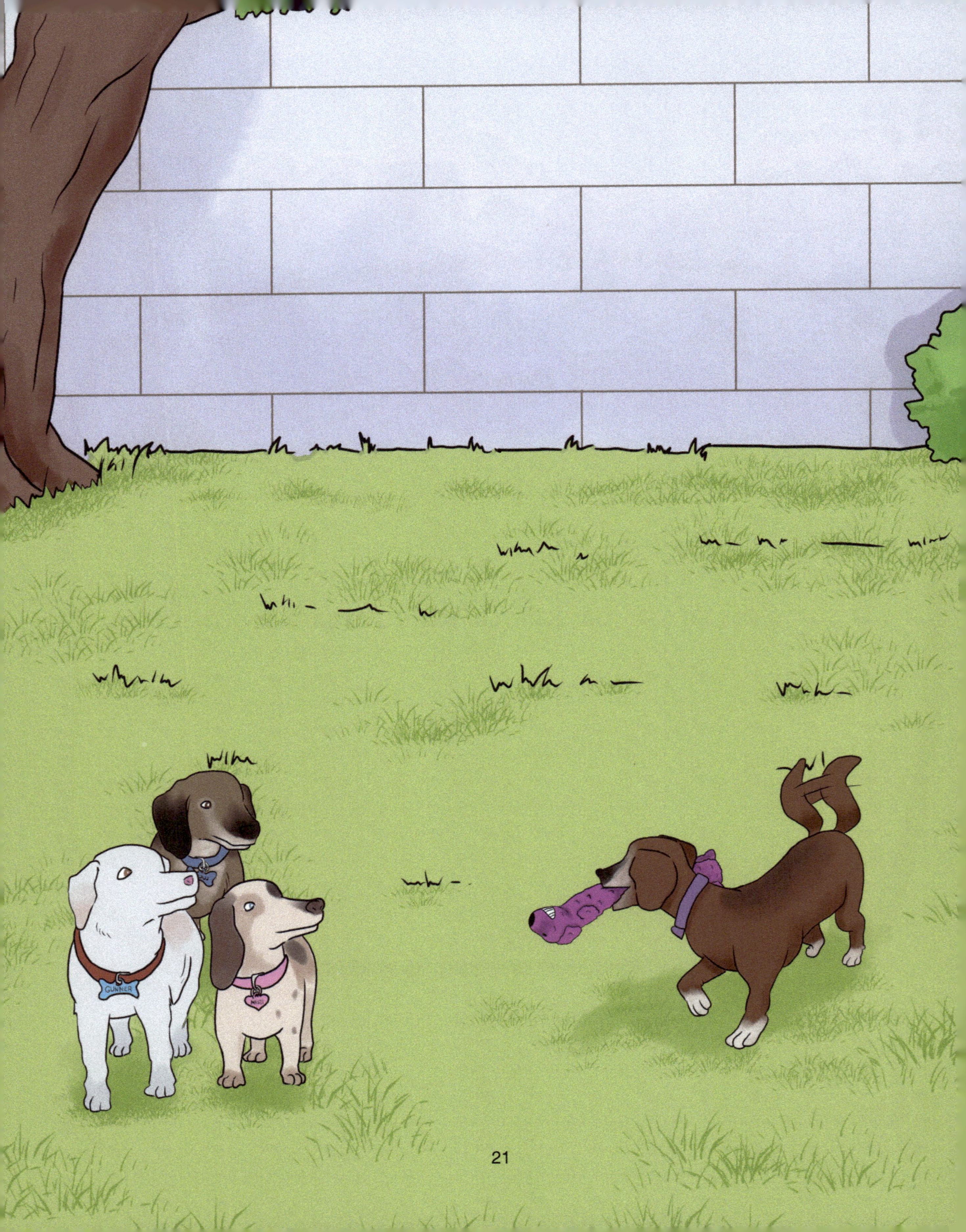
GUNNER
MISTI

Now that we have Lucky, Misti and Gunner, we have to keep an eye on Gracie's woobie. They want to shred it to get to the squeaker and the stuffing. This makes Gracie very unhappy.

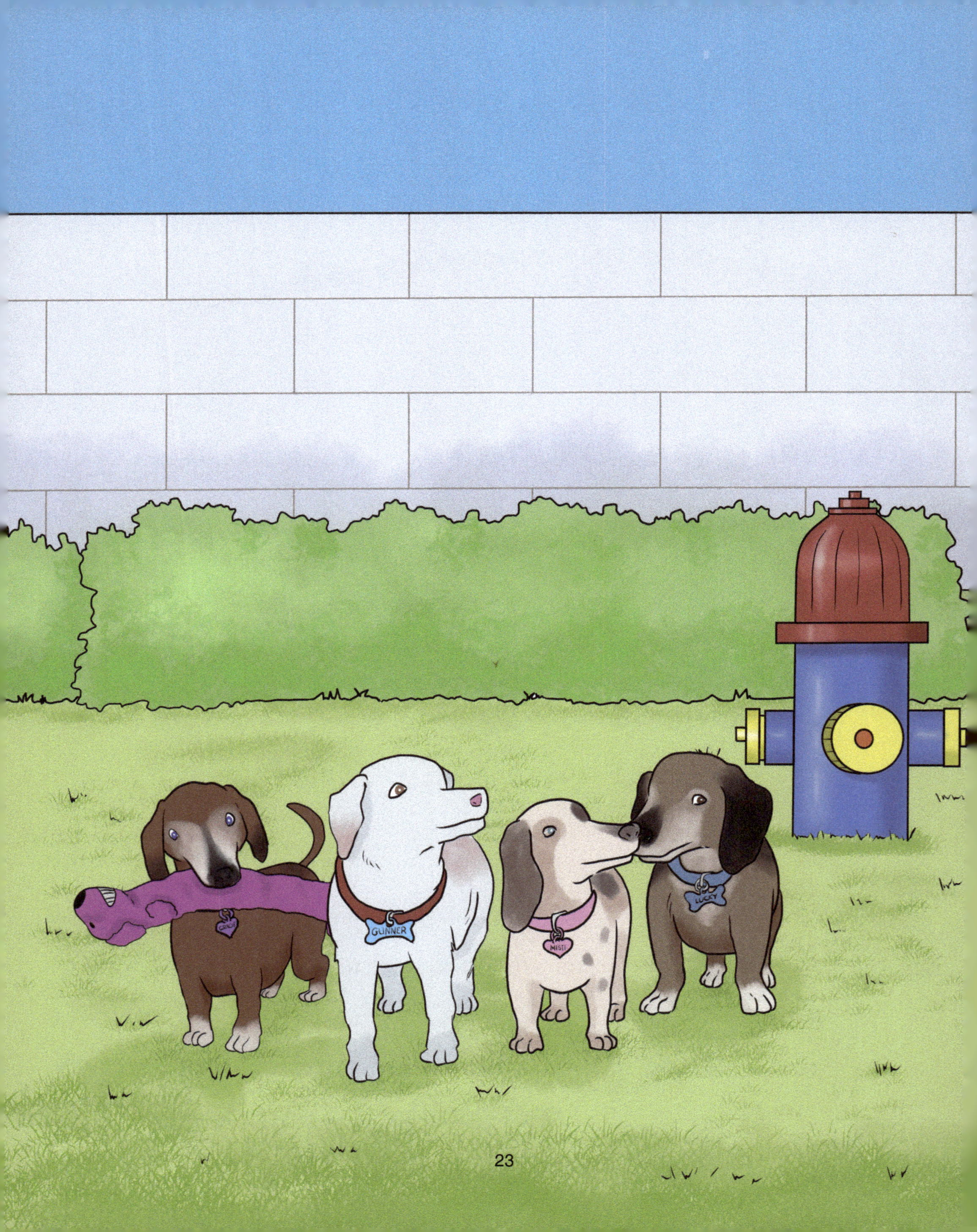
GUNNER
MISTI
LUCKY

Gracie now has Lucky, Misti, and Gunner, who are also doxies.

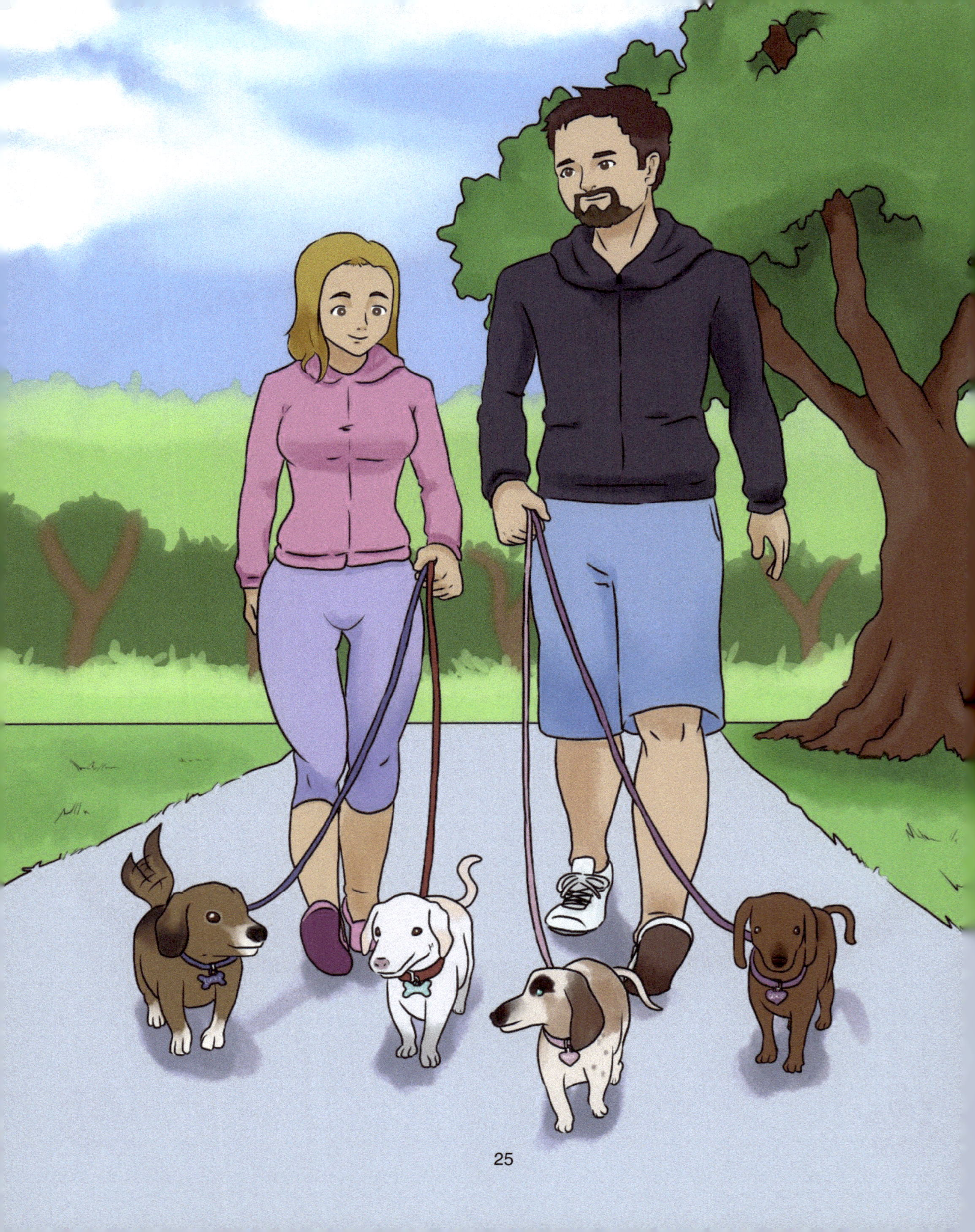

You can read about them in *The Big Adventures of Little Lucky*, *Gunner Gets a Forever Home*, and *Mischievous Misti*.

About the Author

Paula Gehring-Kevish holds a bachelor of science degree as well as a master's degree in school counseling. Two of her passions are animals and children. The Rescue series offers her the chance to write about animals for children. She currently resides in Las Vegas, Nevada, with her husband, Steve. In addition, she has two sons and four grandchildren.

CPSIA information can be obtained
at www.ICGtesting.com
Printed in the USA
BVHW021452180322
631796BV00001B/5